After A Visit
To
A Botanical Garden

Previously from Maggie Harris:

BOOKS

Foreday Morning, 1999
Dancing with Words, 2002
Limbolands. London: Mango, 2004
From Berbice to Broadstairs. London: Mango, 2006.

CDs

Listen to de Riddum
Anansi meets Miss Muffet

For my daughters,
Angie,
Eloise
and
Aimee

Maggie Harris

After a Visit
to a
Botanical Garden

Cane Arrow Press

First published 2010 by
Cane Arrow Press
PO Box 219
Royston
SG8 1AZ

A CIP catalogue record is available from the British Library

ISBN 978-0-9562901-1-3

Cover photo of the author by Marcin Paluch
Front cover by Anim8design [www.anim8design.com]
Printed by Imprint

Acknowledgements:

Some of these poems were previously published in/ on the following :
Equinox; Poui; The SHOp; White House Poets, Limerick website;
'Fragments from the Dark'. Hafan (Women Writing Self and Wales)
The Peepal Tree Anthology 'Red'.

CONTENTS

ONE

AFTER A VISIT TO A BOTANICAL GARDEN

After a visit to a Botanical Garden

This world is mine
dusk comes and *they* depart
rolling away in their torchlight of cars.
This world is mine.

This world is mine.
I glide, breeze past
the darkened pool
the muted rill of swans
the water lilies' heads closed in
their moonlit grey;
I trip lightly on the stones
bent blades of grass
arums' sharp-tongues
hungry, open mouths;
banana parasols, limp,
with trying.

This world is mine.
The children's garden sleeps
I wake him, spin
compact discs on string
conduct new sonatas
for pipistrelles to sing.

This world is mine
my sole academy;
learned Latin graces ears
of darting things on wings
and others sighing, crawling

underfoot, masticating, defecating,
erupting
from their chrysalis like kings.

I seek the walls
the cobbles, stones and flint
the fountains and the glass
those lovely weeping coins
admitting to themselves at last
their predicament.

This world is mine
I, a dancer weaving
in and out of wicker hides
a flautist melting sculpture's steel,
a vortex; spidered vision in the glasshouse
splintering a million prisms

o plantlings -
pale anaemic you

o diddums -
nestling with your flaccid, shallow roots
into this sterile womb

no sun
no moon
no ants
no worms
no bees

no *them* here now, just I

bow your heads

lift your heads
in daytime when they come
thumbs and noses
camera lenses, sniffing, stroking
your pale necks
o! the colour! the shape! the scent!
the *you* geography!

I alone know the truth of you
the acid burning youth of you
the carnivorousness
disguised between your sepal lips
and pouting petulant pistils.
O velveteen senecio candicans!
O sage green cactus heart of Aloe!

diddums

No protectors here now, just I
no gardeners with gloved fingertip
clocking arterial pipework
around this cervix of glass
no yellow hoses raining
no chemists
no scientists no technicians
modulating, cosseting, procreating
your perfect microcosmic world
your Babylonian Eden.

Here is just the night
and you and I
this world is mine.

Saplings

Let me tell you about trees
Poplar and spruce, birch, beech and oak, elm
They're aching to touch the sky, aching, I tell you
To shake the dirt off their feet and fly
What they really want to be are birds and clouds
So they entice them into their big hair
Enticing them with promises of comfort
Wishing to hold them fast, those restless things

Let me tell you about these trees here, outside my window
Pretending not to notice us watching them
Cat-walkers of the world, elegant limbs
And freckled skin, roots like high-heels spiralling
They're set up for the shot, posing with breath-taking angularity
Opaque eyes staring into middle distance
Putting up with the mallards' rub and scratch
The squirrels' endless fitness training

But the saplings now – watch them reach, baby-soft, greedy
Towards each other, each new thing
They're not so concerned about the birds, or clouds
But light, and finding a shape which fits
Just like these young voices chattering around this front room
All Bacardi Breezers and ice-cream
Only now waking up to the pleasures of the night
Not giving a jot, for the awkwardness of morning

Tell me Garden, what are you whispering?

(inspired by Wilson Harris, Vita Sackville-West and Sissinghurst Gardens, after a project for Kent Big Read)

Are you missing the touch of her hands pulling and clearing,
grafting and soothing?
Are you missing the mist of her breath warming and cooling,
fanning, be-dewing?
Are you missing the tread of her footsteps, sturdy or sinking,
leather on slabs, worn soles on wet grass?
Or is it her voice, feeding through the hedges, dancing along
walls,
laughter spores falling on your leaves like rain?

Well worry not; watch as these children curl their young
tongues round Latin names,
implanting words like seeds;
watch as these gardeners enjoy a brief respite, lampooning
snowballs with gloved
hands that grip garden forks, push wheelbarrows,
stock the compost heap, smear condensation from greenhouse
glass, edge seedlings
into starter pots and nursery boxes.
You're not whispering at all but clamouring; pealing away from
every bud and thorn
with such a chorus, that my ears are alive with the ringing.

Wild

And whilst you're on your knees
Clearing, digging, dead-heading
Pulling out stones from in-between the toes
Of your precious plants

And whilst you're cutting back, trimming
Clipping and stripping this year's growth
Of clematis
Bramble
Rose

And whilst you're hoeing, raking, mowing
Aerating, composting, sprinkling fertiliser
Between the avaricious teeth
Of what lies beneath

And whilst you're sitting back contemplating
That June-smooth lawn
The sculpted raised bed, the oscillating
Perfection of stamen, pistil, petal

The blue heads of hydrangea,

Please note: they're all just playing dead
And whilst you turn your contented head
Return the tools to the garden shed
Tread indoors for tea and bed

They'll be at it again,
Seeding, popping, pollinating
Budding, growing, spreading
Their licentious selves
Over the bloody border.

Montbretia, Co Clare

August. And she crowns the hedges
a riot of citrus, blood orange, scarlet.
And you want to gather her up
smother her to your chest
her and all her ladies
tripping into your front room
chorus girls giggling in a teenage fit
of shy bosoms and febrile arms.

Right from that moment you stopped the car
the rain lifting, the one beside you pointing
at the rainbow just forming,
you're gathering armfuls; for close up
she is so tiny and not the same alone
so her sisters come too.
And you wonder it's only sorrow you feel,
how unwillingly she comes
her soft head bobbing like a child's.

Looking Slantwise

Autumn, and the leaves are falling
like the head of my lover into my lap's
billowing fold of cotton.

This is the season for gathering,
for storing and coddling, preserving;
for looking slantwise

at the underside of leaves,
at shadows lengthening
like a cat in the sun.

It is a time for hands,
and a time for utterance,
for tracing the furrows of time

between frown-lines, even
as a promise (or memory)
quickens beneath his cheek.

Montbretia, Wales

In search of poetry I wandered Ireland,
head full of myth and mist,
Boland, Heaney, Kennelly …
and girls with Cork and Kerry accents
slipping out of cars on narrow country roads
to tumble through hedgerows in search of wrecks.

Their laughter sliced the air like bees
and lens foreshortened squares of blue
over heads of corn through singing stable doors
askew with age and longing.
And there you were…
shot through with summer, rampant in the hedgerow

gold with song. And I sang, *Belong.*

I gathered up your name
and a miniature bouquet
to press between words as yet unsung.

And your name came back to me
when islands later on
I stumbled on this garden wild with sheaves
and *you* house-hunted *me*
your leaves precise as spears, your head aflame
with madness, wild, frantic, blazing poetry.

Palm Houses

Away from the chalk faces of Kent I go
looking for palm houses –
Botanical Gardens, black soil, heat falling
like rain down my neck.

I enter, a native daughter, barefoot,
mouth open like a bromeliad,
the hair on my arms rising
like cactus spines.

I must remember I am a guest, must pause to admire
the profusion of colour, the infusion of scent
the architecture of banana leaves etched
like Caribbean parasols on the fine, glass ceiling

They pay me no mind, carry on in their own merry way
The fan-tail palm spreading herself solicitously
The bougainvillea readying herself for a wedding
The fruit flies dancing in the stench of rotting bananas.

Still, I envy those gardeners their intimacy,
their daily frequency into this Cathedral.
They're the first to see the bromeliad open her morning eyes,
the philodendron disentangle his sheen from the vine –

And the palms,
Oh God, the palms…

TWO

PROJECT EXOTICA

Project Exotica

"There is no country which yielded more pleasure to its inhabitants ...
it hath many plains, clear rivers, and abundance ...
Guiana is a country that hath yet her maidenhead..."

Raleigh writing *The Discovery of Guiana (1595),* adding to the
myth of Paradise, El Dorado, *'hills with stones the colour of gold...'*
sailing the land for his Queen.

The transfer of exotica did not quite make it
into the lands of people walking their barefoot walk
in forest which
bit
stung
crawled
sniped
sliced
sucked blood and flesh of
sailors
Cimarrons
plant hunters
pork-knockers
or those simply going along for the vibe.

Virgin. Pristine. Even now the TV crews
mythmaking.

Instead try

dutty brown water
bush
anaconda
piranha
ringworm
Piaiman.

Hear the breadfruit sigh
the water lily rinse her legs in slime
the venus flytrap open her river mouth wide
in the simulation of passion
and in swim the carcasses of desire.

Did he foresee the firstborn fuchsia open her eyes
into a sterile Kew?
The banana, freed from his blanket of blue
tremble in a black hold in a cargo boat
stretch his yellowing self in the aisle
of the Church of Waitrose
alongside

sullen green beans from Kenya
the troubled demeanour of a pawpaw
an agitated pineapple planning her vengeance
for the moment a soft palm will cup her into tomorrow?

Did he foresee Demerara Rum and
Amerindian casryp
smothered in towels and smuggled
through Customs?

Or did his Far Eye dream of high-colour women

propagated by the races of conquerors
ripened like guavas in the sun
imbued by the infusion of reticence
weighed down with gold from Diyaljee's

walking into Bata shoe stores
with the undulating walk of crocodiles
basking their river-soaked skins
under the midday sun?

I, Breadfruit

I, Breadfruit, am Beautyful Bountye
I am Slice of Historye
From Pacific they fetch Me
Carry me roll on wild Sea

I, Breadfruit, am Beautyful Bountye
I hear talk of big City, West Indies
Across far Water, Money Tongue talk
Across far Water, Money Foot walk

I, Breadfruit, am Beautyful Bountye
I am Sustenance, Sea-seasoned and
Withestandyng of Salt
I am Drum too, Boat, Glue

I, Breadfruit am Traveller
Eyes bright and Mouth shut
Am Survivor extra-ordinate
Mister Fletcher, Captaine Bligh

You have writye Me into Historye Booke!

I, Breadfruit, am bound for Stomach of black Men
First Jamaica Man not love Me
Because he not free
Black Men Lip seal like Liberty.

But! There be New Century!
They all learn love I Breadfruit!
I Breadfruit will sing Name
Koqo, Tamaipo, Samoa, Uto Wa

Havana, Aravei, Tatara, Yampae.

For I am Brother Gourd, Calabash of Home
I, Breadfruit be most beautyful Bountye. Aye.

Breadfruit was the cargo on The Bounty, meant for feeding the slaves of Jamaica. When a shipment eventually arrived there, the slaves refused to eat it. Breadfruit is now one of the staple and versatile foods of the Caribbean.

Sonnet for a Portuguese Woman

You wouldn't have cared about ships or seas, apart
from the cargo that mattered – New Zealand butter,
sardines, matches, kerosene.
                              Wartime children
were your concern – oil-slicked, sugary children,

nappy-headed, dust-kneed, forming a litany from
your mouthful of names: *Angelina Carmelita Petronella
Machado. Mother.*
                    Rosary blow-mouth full of incantation
and necessity, never speaking of that other harvest failing,

that buss-ass Madeira harvest
forcing farmers to become sailors and board ships
where crucifixes rusted on collar-salt bones.
No. Just gee-up that donkey-cart there and tell us tales

of a mer-woman washed up on some fresh-water creek in
Demerara
with the know-how of transforming fins into feet.

Tourist Market

Yuh got a small piece fuh me Mistress?
Me nah eat since las Sunday
Me pickney him a starve
See he belly swell out he navel so
Me milk dry up long time…

Ova here! Down here! Yes that's me Sis
Me cyant stand up fuh long see.
Yuh wan pieca pine? Guinep?
Sweet mango? Ow bout a pieca sugarcane?
Yuh cyant get that in Hingland rite?!

English! Hey English! I got a nice gold ring heh
Pure Columbian that's right, bargain jes five EC dollahs
What about some aloe then? Pick fresh dis mawning
Lord! Look how your lady shoulder bunnup!
Wait, Hold on! You walking away from me?
You tunning you back pon me?!
Is that the manners y'all learn in the US?
You prefer spend you money in the Govament shop?
Cheups Man y'all haul yuh rass.

Dear Sir, please to tek this conch here from me
You will pay twice de price on board
No Sir it is not a protected species
Is Lambie we eat Sir.
Madam, this will look nice on your mantlepiece eh?

Come on Sir, I too old to fish now you see
Just $8 Sir. No? 6 then, just $6 it will fit nice
In your suitcase, wrap it in your towel Sir.
The Lord be praised. Bless you Sir, Bless you.
Sir, can I interest you in this nice shell necklace …?

Road is not beach.
Bikini belang on beach.
Road is not deck on board.
Bikini belong on deck, not road.
You walking round my island lika dat?
You would like me to do dat?
You would like me to wear bikini in Tescos
And feel up your plantain like dat?
Have a nice day Madam.
Go lang you way.

     Y'all having a nice time?
     Havana is a beautiful city, you enjoying her?
     You staying long? I could show you round
     There is a lot of people like to take advantage.
     But I have specialist knowledge,
     I 'm a university professor you know
     And times are extremely hard

Please don't walk away from me Sir
Please don't walk away from me
     Please don't walk away
        Don't walk away

Ancestor on the Auction Block
(after a poem by Vera Bell)

So you:
      around whom I've circumnavigated my entire journey
having to be sailor, archaeologist, map-reader, ventriloquist
      dredging, sifting, navigating, alliterating -

I will not repeat here the journeys of others
      will not imagine or re-imagine you, bestow upon you
whatever 'voice' they believe to be yours.

No.
      We know well the scene: the pen or market square, an
indoor arena
out of the rain, the prising open of jaws, the peeling apart
      of vaginal lips.

Let me instead address that hammer still speaking today
      still rising in men's fists over the price of women
veiled in condescension, satire, jest

whilst even I, whose words journey on without me
      have, stamped indelibly beneath my skin:
Descendant. Colonies.

Meditation

There's a brown girl in the ring falalalala
A brown girl in the ring falalalalala...

Let me do a meditation on skin
Skin.

Let me do a meditation on tongues
Tongues clicking Xhosa, tongue nailed to a gatepost.

Let me do a meditation on eyes
Eyes calabash-brown drowning in the blue from a Dutchman.

Let me do a meditation on hands
Hands smoothed over bottom whipped by licks, plantation
kisses, Brixton boys hungry for Caribbean ass.

Let me do a meditation on ears
Ears seduced by Kyrie Eleisons, rock steady, Jimmy Cliff, a lover
whispering just a little finger in your panties sweetness, Dylan
Thomas, djembe beat.

Let me do a meditation on noses
Noses pulled straight into European beauty, assailed by
patchouli circa 1972 in a Kingston (upon Thames) dancehall,
Led Zep and Yes and ganga shared in a purple painted bedsit
Richmond, Surrey.

Let me do a meditation on legs show me you motion, arms
limbo baby, breasts the bounty and burden babies of.

Born into this community of corpuscles also:

One African elephant
tired of the love of his keeper after twenty-three years
tired of his body endlessly bathed with Southern water and
Kentish mud
tired of millions of gallons of piss running down a concrete yard
in the enclosure
dreaming of waterholes and plains
remembering waterholes and plains
swings his trunk like a cannon
and guns his keeper down.

Being

If words were all that language is
how simple it would be
to speak of sapodillas ripening
the texture of their skin

That woman there remembering
Soufriere, small boys diving
skin rippling like seals
beneath the shadow of the Pitons

watching this hillside now where
the llamas no longer tremble
as fighter jets come screaming
but turn their lovely eyes

towards the stile.

THREE

SETTING SEED

I come from

I come from borrowed names, given names, names of dis-
possession
Hawker, Harris, Princess *Margaret* waving her white-gloved
hand
from the motor cavalcade.
I come from faces, earth & sun faces, tamarind faces,
watermelon teeth.
From hands: rough carpenter's hands, smooth Nivea-creamed
hands, blue-veined & cutexed, hands that reached for the cane.
I come from skin & bone, Portuguese skin, African bones, buried
in forgotten oceans,
I come from trade.

I come
from the ringing of bells, the clapping of hands
from foreday morning drums over a Pentecostal backyard
from cutlasses and ships
from red bauxite pyramids of barges
from that name, *Captain*, cutting through those rivers
they charted, navigated, christened, 'Home'
I come from the wind.

I come from dreams of paradise

From dreams of paradise I came.

This poem was inspired by one of the same name by Jo Roach.

Blue-eyed Guyana Boy

I wanted to write about Donald
whose blue eyes were left on the road
that Corentyne Highway, in 1984
the young spend their time looking forward
the old looking back; whilst my vision's
still sharp, let me think on

That country boy in a family of girls
his Mammee crouched over the kerosene stove
his Da on the front porch, reflecting
on returnees bringing their voices back
from over the seas, in a flash of black leather
and a grip of new clothes.

The porch looked out on that road
once a track where cartwheels turned
bearing broken limbs of sugar-cane.
Then tarmac came, and speed,
motorbikes and diesel, country buses
full with folks greedy for civilization.

Buses with names on the side,
Conqueror, or *Justify*, loud music
and jewellery blazing, just like the one
that cut him down that school morning.

And I'm thinking of all the things he's missed:
the first MacDonalds, the pull of a fag,
the feel of girls, hip-hop.
Then there's others: guns and knives,

Race; that last the hardest, seeing as
Mammee's fadda fadda had shipped in from Madras

and Da's dadda dadda had left Accra in chains
and somewhere too, along the line
blue eyes had rolled down Plantation Hill
from some English second son.

That golden skin, that tamarind skin
that mud-brown, calabash, red-earth skin
would have been sliced to ribbons just defending;
and I wouldn't remember him now
a generation and an ocean later,
a flash of white teeth and blue eyes shining
as he fetched me a bucket to bathe that time
I brought my grip
to their Corentyne front door.

Havana

I dreamed you ...

... skin peeling
conquistador-gold, cupolas,
columns, colonnades

cutting long shadows
on cobbles. Dogs hound the cool
of stone, the gothic doorways

where Moorish oases
of date-palms and fountains
beckon.

Green-blazered waiters
ease platters between
red elbows

and the curl
of black
wrought-iron.

I walk, past plaster-dust
and rubble, masonry four centuries
tired of standing

of being stood, of being;
steel girders
courtesy of Unesco

rippling with the backs
of workers plastering foundation
between the cracks.

Ashamed, I stare
through a doorway
framing an old man's bed,

his thin feet resting on cardboard

rescued from the street.

xxx

On the cobbles a maitre d wanders
menu in hand
honey to the tourist hive

raising their stung necks upwards
at spires and balconies
a sky blue as cobalt.

Mojito?

xxx

Mid-morning: in the upper
courtyard of the Valencia Hotel;
the gardener drenches

the crotons from a dented
watering-can; the yucca
and the ginger-lily

wait, watching
the water run on the tiles
sunlight slash through

transparent leaves, the maid wheel
her trolley of white linen
through ten-foot

Jamaica Wood doors;

their leaves bend to the clumsy
Hola!
of the new arrivals.

    xxx

... the Arab restaurant
in Calle de Mercedes ...
through the couscous and the lamb

the trio on guitars, the parrot in the vines
the caged lovebirds, a crying Canadian
child,

one Rhode Island Red runs,
hungry
for your fingers.

They're hungry for you
too, out there on the street, hungry
for tourist dollars

hungry for conversation
conversion, convertibles,
cigars of *banana leaves*

curled in tight bouquets
of white paper, carried hopefully
beneath the arms of aged

men and women
circling aisles and patio pews
the shadow of the cathedral.

Hungry;

even those birds of paradise
sweeping the square in crimson taffeta
paper flowers, photographers and kisses,

hungry.

And hunger meets in a place
patrolled by the guards
dressed in that particular green

favoured by revolutionaries,

guarding the entrances to hotels,
the Plaza Vieja, glass-fronted
perfumed stores whose

top-notch merchandise
belies the embargo; but
turn another corner,

another shady street
pavement worn with the heat
of plastic shoes, pass by

the Cuban store for Cubans –

its bare shelves of milk powder
rationed rice and bread, black beans,
a kilo of chicken.

Havana,

      I had dreamed you
like so many others before me
and on that fast road from the airport

excitement fuelled my blood
like a drug; diesel and dust
and the dry romance

of clapped out cars and smoke-
propelled exhausts were no match
for the clatter of my heart,

neither was your cracked face.

The breath of the Caribbean,
the prince's kiss.
I sleep.

Georgetown Girls, 1969

… swinging from bar stools
sunbrown legs in high heel shoes
Cutex toenails red as lipstick
Avon Calling! by canoe
across the Demerara river

Georgetown girls and chocolate milkshake
Babycham and low-cut frocks
Creole earrings, nugget rings
Guyana bangles dangling

They know the lime they have the style
The movies taught them how to smile
 At good time guys and guys who'll fly
Them out to cadillacs and weddings

Others burn the candle low, the light bill high
book learning. And offices
and babies wait
to interrupt their lives.

But for this brief time these girls
from Bishops High, St Rose's …
swing sunbrown legs from tall bar stools
in high heel shoes and Cutex toe-

nails red as kisses
Avon caught them ripe
before the falling.

Importing Rainstorm

(*Rainstorm*, an Eve tale from the Amerindians of Guyana.

There are other goddesses
besides the ones you know

let me free one from the slipway of my tongue

Rainstorm.

She fell, like Alice
through pre-El Dorado sky

following her breech-birth feet onto a land of plenty

Rainstorm.

She fed, she fed
laced her tongue with hassa fish, labba deer

roamed that land of green pastures and roaring waterfalls

Rainstorm.

earth as yet un-named
but soon to be, *Guiana, land of many waters*

Rainstorm.

let me release her name from the slipway of my tongue
position her onto the sea of memory
where other names *Wapishana, Wai-Wai, Macusi*

slide canoes from beneath the sigh of trees
the clutch of forest
leap of jaguar

she fed, she fed
and, buttocks fleshed with bounty climbed for home

to meet the fate of travellers whose journeys mark them, flesh them
fuller than the birth canal

and cry, she cried
between two worlds she cried, endless tears of Paradise
and plenty

You never see commotion so!
eye-water pouring down
mash up she eye and stamp down she foot
wriggle that side, writhe odder side
holler and holler till clouds bust apart
eye-water shake coconut tree
make rapids overflow
make waterfall to hell and go -
Kaieteur! Mazaruni! Potaro!

So now when it rain everybody say -
that girl Rainstorm, she crying again!
That girl Rainstorm, she crying again.

Stuck fast between two worlds, Rainstorm
a woman rippling with the tribulations of her country
Land of Many Waters for true true.

Red: Another Song for Daddy

Pirate Ship, St Lucia, 1999

That girl in St Lucia recognising me -
"Red girl!"
(The nose and mouth? The Guyanese bangles?)

In my longing my heart blipped like a monitor -
in all this Caribbean sea
some small-island girl should know
we shared a history

and even on the sailing ship
I walked the plank between
the black boys on the rigging
and the tourists bright white teeth.

St. Rose's High School, Guyana, 1965

There is nothing like a red ant bite
that sharp, recognizable sting
that has you jumping up in rage
beating the back of your skirt
like one possessed

and you don't know which is worse
that you be condemned to hell
by one so small, or lose your cool
in front of posh girls
one hot school afternoon

Scholarship girl, courtesy of
The Reynolds Metals Company;
country-girl a-come to city.
My tongue swelled up
and refused me the luxury of speaking

right through to '66.

Red Pepper

Bring me a bag of peppers
and I'll tell you their names -
piri-piri and pimento
jalapeno, chilli, capsicum

the smallest are the hottest: bird pepper
they will linger at the back of your throat
small guns blazing
refusing to be extinguished
by mere water

xxx

And should I even attempt to speak
of hibiscus petals
scarlet as that fever
that bore her to her death
as flushed as a new poem
on its way to becoming?

Or of birds whose very plumage
was their undoing
gracing hats and quills,
collectors' glass boxes
disappearing into graveyards
they christened
Museums.

Red Man
All this you must know, Daddy mine

up with the dawn of a Berbice morning
navigating the arteries of rivers.

You sail into the foreday morning of my sleep
just as you steered *The Manhattan, The Radio City,
The Maracaibo*

down the river like a king
your bauxite cargo pyramids
glowing from flat-bottomed barges.

I don't know what you knew of alchemy,
that process that turned red dust into metal
aluminium, hulls, tin foil

only that
you emerge from beneath the canopy of trees
themselves bleeding

> *hard to believe that trees like these
> are trembling far below the knees
> on anklebones the hue of stones*

> *and toenails curling crumbed earth*
> *knowing well its own fragility*

the captain *red*/man sailing *red*/river
of blood and memory to scrape the *red*/earth
clean of rainforest trees

but what was on your mind but the pay cheque
your four daughters, your wife
school uniforms, the light bill
a bottle of XM Rum?

Between that red dust and me
one river, one sea, one ocean
innumerable lives
intersecting, breaking away into tributaries
migrating flat-footed people
from continents into cities
cold, dull grey.

Emerging from the rain-forest
in tin-can glory

knowing about sandbanks waiting beneath the tides
and kerosene lamps swinging in a red-eye dusk

one Captain, *Aye*
a black man emerging
from that core
that beating, pulsing core
of darkness.

ABC with Michael Jackson

When Michael Jackson died I remembered that first time
hearing *ABC*
the high-pitched tone bursting through the monogram
of gold, the Phillips radio.
A Lickle Boy, ee's jus' a lickle boy the adults said.
Then radio was the Voice, we gathered
on the steps and listened as the world came singing in.
News of Kennedy had travelled so, and Marilyn Monroe
and long haired boys called Beatles whom our parents,
warm to Elvis and Jim Reeves, could not believe.
And they could not believe that small black boy
with the high-pitch voice in a world where black
had to fight for the right to sing
- Nat King Cole, Louis Armstrong, Belafonte -
and where amongst Calypso, Lata Mangeskar,
Hymns and Death Announcements,
we children listened to Burl Ives, *The Little White Bull*
and *When Santa comes down the chimney.*

He gave us back the music,
wrested it from those to whom music had belonged
and our neighbours held their heads up high
and stroked their curly-headed children saying
yall children listen -
if a lickle black boy can light up America who knows what we can do?

Our history there on back-steps built by slavery's labouring
hands
was liberated then, echoed by the nursery school next door
chanting *ABC,* boys and girls of every race before they learnt
to read, to write, to take their place.

44

Plantation Children

When they took the first one she howled
Her screams bent the young cane leaves
Twisted the green shoots
Lifted their hungry roots

When they took the second her cries
Rose up to the clouds, woke Rainstorm
From her slumber, brought
Showers tumbling down

With the third her sobs rolled backwards
Into her throat, drowned there
By the fourth and fifth
Her heart had become a stone

FOUR

FLOWERING

Madonna of the Afterbirth

There is no pain
like the pain of daughters
leaving

especially in these barren times
of little or no ceremony.

No betrothals, no fattened goat
no head of cattle or bridal tent
nor twenty-five carat worth of intention.

The world steals them away bit by bit
teachers, friends and lovers
bearing them further and further away

from the Madonna of the afterbirth.

Passion no longer lies

Passion no longer lies between these sheets

If the walls could speak, the bedsprings whisper
they would tell of a time when he stayed over
with his sly smile and his oiled limbs and
that long experimental tongue

In the beginning he fell from the thin pages
of books, from lips as far away as lamp-posts
from the strings of guitars, the
syrup of radios, alighting like mosquitoes on

polished timber, hot concrete, the soft uncurl of ears

he travelled on the roads of spice, the veil
of incense, on laughter pungent with travel
in reptilian shoes dulled with time and maybe
it's time herself who culled him

so that now he waits like a lizard on a fence
precipitating movement, frozen in the dark night,
tight with the fear of the passage
of fingers across his skin.

Grandmothers of the Morning

Mama

dying slowly in that Berbice bedroom
images of the worlds she'd known
flickering behind darkening eyes -
the river in the mosquito season
high tide on the sandbank
the morning light clean
as Columbus' sword

a bevy of bats in the mango tree
fireflies above the porch
a kerosene lamp swinging
Massa's cold blue eyes

Read me that passage again, Jimbo boy
that verse from Solomon

Mother

Through the waves of the morning tide
her dead sister's head breaks
why you left mih girl child?
only tek the boy -
fetch she, fetch she o sister mine
or is haunt I gon haunt you
till kingdom time

Portuguese woman
Black man at her side

rises and gathers Demerara children
into the brown Berbice

land of many waters

Mummy

mermaids have no place by the mangle
only maids
with hands wiry and unclasped
unlike yours welded in prayer

Gene Pitney and Jesus on the airwaves
A town without pity
evangelical, those red fifties
colouring your vision

so even now, decades later
the thought of Cuba
fills you with rage

Me

remembering hallelujahs hurled across a morning
and wearing grand-daughters' kisses on my face
I board a flight to Havana.

Poem from a Lost Mother

Just pretend I've died
as the grass does, or the leaves
from a hot dry summer, or from autumn's disease.

Just pretend we have no history
don't share blood, or lungs
the same-shaped lips, jealousy or lies

that we are strangers in this world
that you were born washed up on a shore
with soft sterile bones

on a pyre of embers, that might well be the residue of stars.

Pass me casually in the street, as one does
a dog, or a tree, and forget laughter
trapped in the hedges, or palm-prints on a wall.

That would explain why my cries circle
this empty landscape like a gull,
and return to me on the wing

and why, one day, your children will prise aged palms
apart like a clam shell
and seek words like these:

labba, marabunta, mother.

Elemental

My daughter, I see you dance and remember …

… retrace fleeting, galvanic leylines of memory …
the earth and I are dancing, speaking, singing
the air and rain … I am volts of electrical blue.

Those days they gave dances names - *rock steady, reggae, ska,*
locomotion, the moon walk, the samba, the cha cha cha.
See your mother there, a feather, a flame, a shape shifter in the
dust,
a scorcher on the dance floor.

The music fuses her feet to the earth, sweat like a volley of lava
runs the ocean floor, cuts through rock, erupts to the sounds
of drums and tambourines, steel strings, backyards, mouth
organs, flutes...

She has forgotten her thin legs, *that* mouth
that hair, the imprint of ancestry, the eyes like those of Dutch
ghosts,
the half-white skin. There are those beyond the circle sniffing
their poison into the air:

this heathen, throwback stuff.
God forgive them, Devil children! Crawling out of their
ghettoes to dance like this…!

Like the sulphur springs of Soufriere, I unlock a world of
tension
 … if not the whole world would explode

those plates on the ocean floor ready anytime
to summon a tsunami.

Roll on the dancehalls, the street parades, festivals,
nightclubbing;
the day will come when you will know that current charging
through arms, hips, bones, and flesh is the soul recognising
itself, celebrating itself through continents, amniotic oceans,
earth, sky, eternity.

Square Dancing

Remember that square in Kilrush, Co Clare
folk violins in the rain?
The town was out dancing
the dance caller hailing
another two for the frame.

Square-shouldered we stood by the side of the road
and watched as they danced -
old men of eighty, young girls of ten
waltzing, reeling, twirling.

So I turned to you and I said, My love
Will you dance with me?
But your eyes were far and your voice was cold
I don't dance, you said

So my dreams lay down on the stones there
the whole of the moon in my eyes
while they danced, they danced
right over my bones
through the shawl I'd worn
for the night.
They danced, they danced
in their strong country boots
they danced in their silver-heeled shoes
they danced, they danced
in the blue moonlight
right through the pores of my skin.

And I turned and saw her there with you
there by the side of the road
her whole head staring into the dance
her eyes so wild I called and called
to join me into the rhythm they bled
under the stones of their shoes.

But it was not you and it was not me
I don't dance, you said
and I stood in the rain and watched them spin
in that square in Kilrush, Co Clare.

The Auction Rooms

Rising like a well-spring
like vomit,
upwards through heart and bone
burning the chest,
the back of the throat,
desire.

Glass, oak, mahogany
marble-smooth and grained
scored by the thumb-prints
of centuries
the memory of eau-de-cologne,
damask, brocade.

In parkas and black leather
sharp-eyed as owls
hands run over veneer,
lifting, stroking, estimating;
spirits, pulses, ears alive
to the auctioneer's volley

ricocheting, ascending;
then

one long crazy moment of levitation

before the fall
of the hammer
to the silent laughter
of lounging, departed souls.

Vampire Love Song

Let me love you like the sweet drop of a sparrow-hawk
On a night heavy with stars, under a bellied moon

Your body is white beneath me, the waxed sheen of camellias
A cello in contour, *el fragrante, deliciosa, mea culpa* ...

The creatures of the night have dispersed at my descent
Away into undergrowth and tunnels of earth

Their many hearts thump away beneath us, uneven
and frantic as yours.

O what a night, what a Saturday night!
What lured you, intoxicated and laughing, out from the ray

Of the street lamp - the shortcut home?
Or did you scent me, sense me, my waiting breathlessness

My own heart racing away like the mille-second beat of a
Hummingbird's wings?!
O my darling, my darling! I draw you in, drink you in

So humbly, so adoringly, with a man's mouth, a man's lips
A man's tongue... And how willingly you rise and fall

To the tremble of my own fast-flushing fingers
Honouring you, worshipping you, breast, bone, throat.

I'm not complaining

It's nice that you bring me tea
when I'm half-awake and half-asleep
that you ask me how I am today,
it's nice to know you care
and I'm not complaining.

It's great to hear you on the phone
your charm , your grace, your business tone
your plans for bringing the bacon home
a woman couldn't ask for more
and I'm not complaining.

You know the name of every bird
it's habitat, its special call,
we're driving and you see a kite
rock the car and check its flight
but I'm not complaining.

It's just that now and then
I wish that I could wake to find
your lips are travelling on my thigh
to places that as yet have no horizon.

I dream that you would frame my face
beneath your open, winged hands;
for beneath this skin, beneath these bones
a small cerulean bird is trying to sing.

You may say I'm self-obsessed
trapped in a time that's been and gone
before Sunday morning tea and toast
echoed the Holy Ghost, or the memories
of small children at the table;

a time when you circumnavigated me
from breast to throat, with hands, with oaths
our bodies wrecked like broken boats
and no-one cared whether we were afloat
or drowning.

Now, caught between these residues
of promised lands and open skies
I wait, but please don't think
that I'm complaining.

Wedding Poem

Love is of man's life a thing apart, tis a woman's whole existence
                                        Alfred, Lord Tennyson

My daughter,
Look at you now, shimmering like diamonds, like dawn
Sparkling
On a waterfall
Crystals and lace adorn you, light glows from your skin.

This walk you've walked, these long steps up the aisle
A childhood away from those first tiny steps, on pointy toes
Around the sofa.

You danced before you walked, before your birth
Strummed my skin like a tambourine, pointed your toes
Stood at five months on feet reminiscent of mine,
Always rushing to encounter life.
And danced you danced, from ring a roses to ballet
And beautiful you grew and tall you grew and stumbled
As we do, on stones and bends in the road
Growing armour to combat this crazy world.
And on becoming a mother your arms curved to enclose your
Babies
As I once enclosed you.

Turns and twists in the road have led you here
Up this silver path shimmering in the light of hope
Escorted by a host of butterflies.
And I say: Praise be!

For you are like new things, polished and glistening
You, my new son, with the strength of youth
The bravery of youth, truth and earnest conviction
Boy and man, father and traveller.
Prove Tennyson wrong; for love is not just a woman's 'thing'
Love should not be 'of man's life a thing apart'
But wholly so;
For love is the breath of life, the joy of children
The comfort at the end of the day .

So Praise be! this special day, this longed-for, planned-for day
Where hope shimmers like a host of butterflies.
Praise be! to your new life.
Praise be.

FIVE

BRANCHING

Creation Song

For the students of Clarendon House School, Ramsgate, on the opening of their new Art Centre, 2008

This is the place where peacocks call
Where dreams grow tall
Where the soul and mind will learn to fly

These floors, this glass, this ceiling high
Each brick, each stone will be a guide
Each hand that smoothed, each hand that filed

Each wheel that turned, each spark that burned
Each individual dream, has forged this lock
This key, this door that opens now for you.

This is the place where words will journey side by side
With movement, shape and colour, jump and jive
Each note composed, each pirouette, each lyric
Song and sonnet, Dali, Shakespeare, Monet
Kahlo. Real and relative, will take your hand
Inspire that need centred deep within us
To sing to dance to dramatise, to paint the sky, inscribe
Like those so long ago, with brush and stick and stone
On walls, in caves, with blood and bone.

This is the place where peacocks call
Where dreams grow tall
Where the soul and mind will learn to fly.

Girls Waiting

Winchester.
Girlies. Jewelled bellies. Rhinestone bangles from River Island. Flip flops already though it's only April. They're going shopping, are counting their money on the platform in-between texts to someone called Maddy who's late and will meet them lata in Woking. Their heads are from a Russian triptych, dull gold curls precisely curled from shared tongs back in a bedroom that I know will be ankle-deep in tops and shorts and tights and shoes and cardies and Clearasil wipes and a drawer spilling out with thongs and bras and necklaces just like the ones they'll be bringing home later to add to the pile and find they'd left the tongs plugged in and it had burned a hole right through the carpet.

Sittingbourne.
And I said to im I said don't you tek the bleeding piss outa me come round my gaff drink my booze eat my food tek ova the remote as if you own it. My kids ave ad enuff of fellas like you teking ova dere ome fer its dere ome an all innit an ow come you think you can slide yer feet unda my sofa jes like dat ... an yeah I know yeah rite dats jes wot Stace said but they neva blinkin listen do dey ... anyroad one o dere dad's getting out dis week an dats why im waitin ere see bound to be on dis train from Sheerness have to lead him off rite God help me when e finds out!

Birmingham New Street.
Red sari, red bag, pacing. Full length of platform, pacing. One two, one two, measured steps, eyes straight ahead. To the end of the platform, pause, look down the track, turn around, walk back, pace.

Trains pull in and out, suits pour out of electric doors, surge onto the platform, wash over her, red buoy on the surf, recede, rise up the escalator. Brief moments the platform is hers again. She glides like a dhow, cutting her sure way through the current.

Southampton Central. Platform 1.
Black and gorgeous she is. Striding, straightened bob bouncing, sleek and shiny Diana Ross circa 1976. Miss Black America. Wide smile and cocoa-butter skin, head high, shoulders back. Imagine her in those magazine ads selling face creams: *What are YOU waiting for?* Jacket sleek over the hips, long legs. No baggage, just the handbag. I wonder at her destination. But she heads to the Café Rizzamiz, leans there, smiling as my train pulls out.

I wonder what they're thinking; watching?
Maybe they don't notice me at all.

Of Morte d'Arthur and The Wide Sargasso Sea

This library's not for burning, but caught within a memory
as thin as those pale pages - the Sir Thomas Malory -
Edition? Some distant time to this.
Domestic memory mine, sharpened on *The Wide Sargasso Sea*
another wife gone mad with smells of passion and remembered
heat,
wheeling prams through foreign streets in dead of winter.

Morte d'Arthur, the Malory, I'd whispered, leaning
on the pushchair beneath the librarian's eye, chest tight
with expectancy and fear.
There was a Tennyson on the shelf but no, as if *she* had nothing
else to do but descend into basements; why today, why *these*?
Not taken out since 1938.

Later on the sofa whilst the baby slept, the pages turned,
yellowed as my fingers in this climate … school poetry.
Somewhere in these pages dozed an England offered back
from days of schoolrooms loud with Caribbean prattling -
Lebanese cedars, Tam O'Shanter, Prisoners of Chillon,
lochs and Lochinvars and knights …

and hours passed, between the nappy changing, the heating on
the hob of tins of baby food from Boots - those dreams again -
not this coarse love between the sheets, but Lancelot's, whose
battle-weary fingers stroked my cheeks whilst lyric language
poured
into my ear - not this Southern rasp of *innit*s and *awlrightlove*s
but
silken threads and gossamers and *ye* and *olde* and Avalon and

ladies of
the lake rising like manatees with grace.
If the Catholic was still not deep within me, keep I would have
kept them,
all three - for three they were, that magic fable number, each one
small
and fitting warm within my palm as if they'd made their home
there. Could just imagine one or three white lies -

So sorry, the baby dropped them in the bath, how much were they?

A generation later, returning from the sun, I heard the library
burned,
my heart did too, and fell
from battlements too high for me to rescue, knowing that the
flames rushed
through the basement too, and wondered if the last to take them
out
had been myself, that Ramsgate morning, 1979.

How close I would have held them; how still.

Ramsgate Library burned in 2000

Where Wolves...

wearing the skin of humans he blends into the urban landscape
drives his four by four through the town, laughs with the teller
in the bank
strolls the golf course with the pack, all easy in disguise -
coppers, surveyors, building contractors, publicans -
draft bitter sliding smoothly down designer throats.

soon he will go home to that little girl in the red coat bleeding
into the landscape
remembering how even when he had thrown the stone at her
retreating car she had returned
fuelled by the small face of their son framed in the upstairs
window
and even when his fingered paws had scored a right almost
through her cheekbone
- that cheekbone which in a past life would not have looked out
of place on the cover of Vogue -
and even when the pounding of her size four feet along the
midnight pavement had flicked the light switch of the
neighbours
and even when the police car had purred away re-assured it was
only a domestic
and even when the boy had placed himself between the knife
and his mother's small frame backed up against the kitchen sink
still she returned time and time again putting his howl right
back there in the burning pit of his throat.

xxx

the smell of hunger permeated through the conservatory door
and she recoiled, smelling manworld
in the manacles of steel wrapped around his feet
(*setting the bone*, her daughter said, *car accident*)
manworld in the narrowed eyes, the polish of his teeth.

by his side, her daughter, golden and lovely
casting no shadow, turned thistles soft as cotton buds
returned the sting of nettles into the earth
the anger of wasps into the sky, the thrust of briars
into moss.

would that she had taken him by the throat then
and cast him back out into the wilderness
but light and hope parlayed, dulled them all
whilst the cubs played in the shadow of his smile
until the polish paled, and steel fused to bone.

xxx

this one played the cleverest game
did not come in any disguise, apart from the lack of stealth
walked out in the brightest of lights
women traced their fingertips in the black depths of his coat
laid their white necks at his jaws.

the stories he told walked across the centuries -
his father had *well* prepared him for the world
sharpened his claws on them, tattooed cigarettes
strung them up so they knew how it felt.
No flies on me mate.

brothers surrounded him like a choir, ran to do his bidding
fitted into the layers of his life as smooth as the lifts that glided
up to dancehalls, court rooms, the offices of top barristers.
they were doormen and car salesmen, pimps and advisors,
negotiated
the movement of glory into the veins of the lonely
whilst beneath the cushioned floors
his feet marked crags, fells, valleys.

xxx

how lovely she was! how smooth!
wide her smile, a sophia loren at 14
she bounced onto the stolen leather of his car like a doe
bronzed, gangly, skirt riding pillion on the boned curve of her
hip
school-tie in her shirt pocket, ball point blue
between the bare urge of her nipples.

they yelped when he brought her
lifted their throats at the sun, circled
bathed her with the yellow haze of their eyes

there was down still on her arm, and a breath of milk
his claws slowed as he stroked her
he arched his back, spit.

Xxx

first the freedom to say yes.

the strength to snap the umbilical cord.
a necessary loss of blood, he said, as the trail
between him and her parent's house
stained her passage indelibly.
through the wing mirror he watched the drama unfold again.
he could foretell their every action- teachers, social workers,
priests,
healers from the clean world on the hill, with their wits and
their writs.
and the mother, swaying like a swing bridge between anger and
tears, the flailing of fists; fear.
he would save his smile for her, sometime in the future
she would welcome it.

xxx

new words fell like toys
f… this f…that, *babe.*
champagne cocktails
stretch limos
beads dropped and weighed between fingers -
filigree silver, white gold, cubic zirconia,
Creole earrings from Argos…
>   *they learnt to love the bills best: crisp, new*
>   *then, any condition, milk and nappies don't care*
- go on, treat yourself - he growled -
dropping them onto palms after a night where his claws
tattooed ownership on that supple back.

with my teeth and claws I pleasure you

with the mirror of my eyes
watch me ride the red light
I am Mr. Invincible

xxx

and even when they led him down
keys like the torches of villagers
bright before them
I'll take the laugh anytime he says
waiting for nightfall to slip between the bars
and claim him.

Boy Soldier

He boarded the train to Colchester
Handsome boy, *lovely boy* you could hear
From nans and mums and in the slight smile
From the young girl across the aisle.

Light shone from him, exuberance
Each time the train stopped looked out
Wondering if this was his stop.
He shared his joy with us, asked the way
Disappeared with army kit into the afternoon.

Now sometimes when the TV shows the crowds
Lining the roads of Wootton Bassett
I think of him, and my grandsons
Growing steadily now
Playing war games out in the back garden.

SIX

LIMBO TRAILING

On the Limbo Trail, 1

On the Limbo trail you never know where you will sleep next
On the limbo trail you never know where your eyes will open
Glimpse a ceiling you've never seen before

Contrary to opinion, the spirit does not lead, it follows,
Drags behind like hems in the dust.
It does not like to travel, wants to stay home and raise chickens

Tend a little vegetable plot. It communicates its displeasure
To the body easily.
You get sick.

Cwmpengraig, place of stones

Where yuh navel string bury is not necessarily home
Dis gurl don walk my grandmother say
And walk I walk from Guyana to West Wales
And leave I leave that place of oceans and slave bones
For bruk down cottages and hills where people still pray

And come I come with my forked tongue split syntax
Of Hinglish and street Creole to wander lanes
With no names and no map where even
Sat-nav wuk hard to find being alimbo
Beyond satellite beyond stars

And stars and dreams of stars and songs
Called these Welsh from home
To cross oceans to a continent
Of the imagination

And is peel dis country peel like onion
Garden cups my cottage in its fists of seasons
Caring nothing for my ignorance
Of names, pronunciation, language

And History running in the stream right there
Beneath the stone: mill worker foot-bottom still indent
Ghost voice talking story wild a catchafire
How he catching boat with intention get the hell outa dis place.

It nat fuh him to know some gurl would bring his story
Right back here and tell him tales of sugarcane
And captains tracing latitude and longitude
With quadrant, quill and octopus ink

Is laugh he would laugh true true
whilst that stream keep gurgling,
Stones keep tumbling
Underscore the footfall of my feet.

On the Limbo Trail, 2

Trains. Back in 1959
They ran from Rosignol to Georgetown
Full steam ahead, First Class, Second Class, Third
All had their place, from the coolie woman
With the chickens to the Negro preacher
From Surinam trying to find the English word
For dumplings.
Those little white girls in white socks, white shoes
Leaning out the window, warned to keep
Their arms inside; outside the banana leaves
Disguised bad men with their cutlass ready
To slice arms advertising gold bangles.

From 1972 to 2009 trains changed their style.
(I must not forget to add that we're in England now.)
The carriages with sliding doors, the slide-up windows
The clickety clickety ride on the tracks all
Stepped aside for open-plan streamlined design
Sealed windows and push-button toilet doors
You never really trust will not open and expose
Your backside.

You could still dream though, stare out the window
Watch the countryside and back gardens, fiddle
With the notebook in your hand, eat your sandwich slow
And try your best to ignore the drunk
Singing Cat Stevens loud two seats down.

But then came the mobile phones my dear
And that wonderful refrain, "I'm on the train".

But as well as the interruption into your dreaming
Came the fact that nobody seemed to mind
Sharing all their business with the world.
From who shagged who the night before
To breast implants, to women checking their men
Were coming home for dinner; the most illuminating
That Cardiff girl reading out her bank account number
Cheerily and loudly, then, believe it not,
Her home address.

And so we go, shunted away on runners taking us
From here to there, and in our ears still clickety clack
And in our noses steam
And in our heads dream,
     and dream,
       and dream.

Words across the Water

My daughters walk the deserts of unknowing

My grandmother beating her clothes on a stone
would never have conceived of mobile phones

as neither could Daddy, on MV *Radio City*
property of the Reynolds Bauxite Company.

Only the radio linked the miles, rode the tides.

This is a dry place, a dry dry place

Here are the names of those rivers they shared:
the Berbice, the Kwakwani. Few know them.

Those tales … blood and sugar, women on riverbanks,
the forest waiting, a captain sailing

his tugboat past abandoned plantations
with such beautiful names: Plantation Catherine, Liliengrad…

Beautiful blood-red names.

No amount of megabytes can hold these memories
No battery can charge itself enough

It was the beauty of words that first lured.
El Dorado's sonic whispering, "*Guiana, Land of Many Waters*"

along un-navigable rivers, cutting channels into creeks
and new beliefs: white Gods, Rosicrucians, merpeople,

Currents strong enough to turn, enter oceans
the channel of my sleep.

My daughters walk the deserts of unknowing
This is a dry place. A dry, dry place

Ariel's soft Disney soles never bleed on the shore
in ribbons of blood on jagged stones or glass

No amount of megabytes can hold these memories
No battery can charge itself enough

Alice's tears do not have the force of Rainstorm's
whose seawalls crumble and gutters overflow

and alligators wash
through the villagers doors, and the gun-men killed

that innocent boy just for the price of his mobile.

And where once women waited weeks for the mail-boat
for quinine, and sardines, oil and rope

And where once only the radio played over the sounds
of the rolling waves

my daughters text, my daughters text
in micro-seconds round the globe.

Welsh Llamas

Oh you - coming to greet us over the farm-gate
Your camel-like heads elegant against this Welsh hill-top
Whose sheep graze like commoners beneath your gaze

Your heads turn as one,
Ears - inverted commas, sickles, sweet horns of plenty
Eyes languid behind fringed yashmak of lashes

Peru seems a long way off,
As does Guyana; but for a moment there we shared
An echo between us, of continents.

This Country I Dwell

I have learnt to love myself these past cold years
Trapped here within stone in the shadows of trees
But I am blessed with a mind as sharp as a cutlass
A body ripe as a fallen sapodilla

By day the world looms through glass and the radio
Shards of sunlight, sheets of rain, ferns mimicking
The mambo. Soft shooting daggers of bulbs.

The night-time now, this is the country I dwell
Where the owl hoots to the chorus of my fingers
Where my bones are flutes and I negotiate
Visitations of my dreams.

The midnight robber climbing through the window
Will find me waiting on white sheets infused by the moon
I'll be wearing turquoise at my ears and throat
He will know to meet my eyes

And acknowledge the passage of centuries.

Limbo Trail 3

I used to live here once
(Jean Rhys)

In Broadstairs this summer the sun shined again
the rain fell
the children played by the bandstand
swimming in a pagan heat of dragons.
The Morris men danced.

In the craft tent, the effigies of myth -
Celtic crosses, gold and stone
Welsh slate, curled iron.
Plastic.

I used to live here once.

The view remains the same
sea curling unconcernedly into the bay
faces you have passed for thirty years
searching yours for signs of aging.

The promenade has gone up-tempo
glitzy cafes, gold decking,
glass frontages cloistering their customers
like fragile seedlings from the lick and spit
of the Channel where the galleons still lie
rusting on the seabed's silver trail to El Dorado
Neruda's breath fans this exiled cheek.

In the High Street, Iceland's I believe
is moving into Woolworths.
The shop I bought the bougainvillea
has long since gone. I remember
carrying it like a child, its head of purple turning
this way and that to see where it was going.

In Wales it refuses to flower.
The tree ferns died.

I won't go past the house.
I used to live there once.